Wealth Of Nations

Brazil

Jen Green

HODDER
Wayland

an imprint of Hodder Children's Books

Wealth Of Nations series includes:

Bangladesh   India

Brazil   Nigeria

Cover: Main photo: The cathedral in the capital city of Brasilia.
Inset: A woman from Bahia state, dressed in traditional costume.

Title page: Amerindians peeling manioc in the Amazon.

Contents page: Feeding pigeons in the centre of Brasilia.

Brazil is a simplified version of the title *Brazil* in Wayland's *Economically Developing Countries* series.

Text copyright © 2000 Hodder Wayland
Volume copyright © 2000 Hodder Wayland

Series editor: Polly Goodman

First published in Great Britain in 1995 by Wayland Publishers Ltd. This edition updated and published in 2000 by Hodder Wayland, an imprint of Hodder Children's Books.

A Catalogue record for this book is available from the British Library.

ISBN 0 7502 2591 2

Printed and bound by G. Canale & C. S.p.A. Turin, Italy

Hodder Children's Books
A division of Hodder Headline plc
338 Euston Road, London NW1 3BH

Acknowledgements
All the photographs in this book are by Edward Parker
All map artwork is by Peter Bull.

CONTENTS

INTRODUCTION

Brazil is a giant country in South America. It is the fifth-largest country in the world.

Brazil has a large population, whose ancestors are from all over the world. Some of the people are Amerindian. Ancestors of others are from Africa, or European nations such as Portugal and Italy.

Brazil is a country of great contrasts. It is the world's tenth-richest nation, yet two-thirds of all Brazilians live in poverty.

INDUSTRIES

Brazil has many natural resources. It produces much of the world's coffee, sugar, cotton and cattle, and its thriving factories and mines produce iron ore, tin, steel, cars and weapons.

◀ Many Brazilians, like this accordian-player, are very poor.

▲ Wealthy
Brazilians live
a life of luxury.

RICH AND POOR

However, the profits made by Brazil's industries are not shared equally among its people. Some Brazilians are very wealthy, but most people are poor and do not get proper health care. One-third of all Brazilians do not get enough to eat.

Brazil has the biggest gap between rich and poor people of any country in the world.

LAND AND CLIMATE

▲ Hot, dry desert in the north-east of Brazil.

A VAST COUNTRY

Brazil covers almost half the continent of South America. It shares borders with ten other South American nations, and has the longest coastline of any country in the world.

BRAZIL FACTS

Population: 164 million

Area: 8.6 million square kilometres

Capital city: Brasilia

Language: Portuguese

Currency: Real

Main religion: Catholic (90%)

▼ The land around São Paulo, in the south, is fertile.

MANY LANDSCAPES

Brazil is so large that there are many different types of landscapes and climate across the country.

In the north and west is the Amazon basin, which contains the world's largest rain forest, the Amazon. The climate there is warm and wet.

North of the Amazon basin lie the Guiana Highlands. This mountainous region is partly forested and partly dry. To the south, the River Plate basin is cooler and less forested than the Amazon.

The Brazilian Highlands form a high plateau in the centre of the country. The climate there is tropical and the land is covered by grassland. The coastal strip on the Atlantic shore has a tropical climate with a wet and a dry season.

ONE COUNTRY, MANY PEOPLES

Brazil's population is a mixture of many different races. Today, Europeans, Africans and people of mixed race are the largest groups, but this wasn't always so.

The first people of Brazil were the Amerindians. They have lived in South America for thousands of years. Experts guess there were once between 5 and 10 million Amerindians living in Brazil.

▶ Brazil's children come from many different races.

▲ These children are descended from European and Amerindian ancestors.

PORTUGUESE RULE

Portuguese settlers arrived in Brazil from the 1530s. Between 1500 and 1822, Brazil was a Portuguese colony. The Portuguese mistreated the Amerindians and tried to enslave them. Thousands of Amerindians were killed and many more died from European diseases. Today, about 200,000 Amerindians live in Brazil. That is less than 1 per cent of Brazil's total population.

Many Portuguese men took Amerindian wives and had mixed-race children.

RACE IN BRAZIL	
European	54%
Mixed race	38%
African	6%
Japanese	1%
Amerindian and other	1%

AFRICANS

The Portuguese also made slaves out of millions of Africans, who they brought to Brazil in boat-loads from Africa. Between 1530 and 1850, 5 million slaves were brought to Brazil from countries in West and southern Africa. Each group brought its own language and culture, including music, dance and food.

NEW ARRIVALS

In 1822, Brazil became an independent country. More immigrants began to come to Brazil to settle. In 1850, the slave trade was banned worldwide. Brazil encouraged Europeans to come and work there to replace the slaves. The main groups were Italians, Germans and Spanish, as well as Portuguese.

◀ This building was built by German immigrants in the style of German architecture.

Today Brazil has so many different races it is often called a 'melting pot'. The largest groups are Italians, Portuguese, Spanish and Japanese. There are also many Germans, Poles and people from the Middle East.

In Brazil, it is against the law to discriminate against anyone because of their race or colour. However, prejudice does exist, especially against black people and Amerindians, which is a great problem.

▼ Amerindians in the Amazon rain forest peeling a vegetable called manioc.

WHERE PEOPLE LIVE

Fifty years ago, seven out of ten Brazilians lived in the countryside. Today seven out of ten people live in the cities, and most people live close to the Atlantic coast. In fact, 40 per cent of all Brazilians live in a narrow strip of land which is only 8 per cent of the country.

11

BRAZIL'S WEALTH

Brazil contains extremes of wealth and poverty. Millions of people live in slums called *favelas*, with no running water or electricity. Many people do not get enough to eat. The rich live in luxury flats with private swimming pools. The reasons for these extremes lie in Brazil's history.

▼ This *favela* is in the coastal city of Rio de Janeiro.

COLONIAL TIMES

In the early 1500s, Brazil became a Portuguese colony. French and Portuguese ships sailed to Brazil in search of a valuable timber, called brazilwood. This wood produced a red dye.

Brazil came to be named after the brazilwood trees. Groups of Amerindians traded timber for metal tools and other European goods.

People still ▶ work in harsh conditions on sugar-cane plantations in Brazil.

SUGAR CANE AND MINING

North-east Brazil was an ideal place to grow sugar cane. The Portuguese set up large sugar plantations and forced Amerindians and later African slaves to work there in dreadful conditions.

By the early 1700s, the Portuguese began to explore inland Brazil. They discovered gold at Minas Gerais, in the Brazilian Highlands (see the map on page 24). Soon huge quantities of gold were being shipped to Portugal each year.

BRAZIL'S ECONOMY

Main types of work

Manufacturing	25%
Farming and fishing	11%
Building	7%
Trade and finance	7%
Mining	2%

Gross Domestic Product:
    US$639 billion (1996)

Average yearly income:
    US$3,150 per person

Foreign debt: US$149 billion

INDEPENDENCE

In 1882, Brazil became independent again. The country still depended on mining, and also on farming. The main farm products sold were cattle, coffee and cotton.

From the late 1800s, rubber was needed to make car tyres. Since rubber trees grow in the Amazon rain forest, a rubber industry grew there.

Factories in ► south-east Brazil. Manufacturing industries grew quickly after the Second World War.

▲ A statue of President Kubitschek, who helped Brazil to modernize during the 1950s.

BRAZIL IS MODERNIZED

Until the Second World War, Brazil had bought most of the manufactured goods it needed from foreign countries. These supplies were cut off by the war, so Brazil was forced to develop its own industries.

From the 1950s, Brazil began to industrialize quickly. It also spent money on public projects, such as new roads and power plants.

SOCIAL CONDITIONS IN BRAZIL

- The wealthiest 20% of Brazil's population earn 65% of the country's income. The poorest 20% earn less than 3%. This is the greatest inequality of any country.

- Only 4.5% of Brazil's population owns 81% of the land.

- Brazilian people live to an average age of 66. In Britain, people live to an average age of 76.

- Over 50% of homes in Brazil have no electric lights. 71% have no running water.

- Under 82% of Brazilians can read and write. In Britain this figure is 95%.

DEEP IN DEBT

Brazil borrowed large sums of money from abroad to develop its industries. During the 1970s, its economy grew rapidly. But in the 1980s, foreign countries began to doubt that countries like Brazil would ever pay off their debts, so foreign loans to Brazil stopped.

The country found it had to spend huge amounts of money to repay its debts. It could no longer spend money on public projects such as hospitals and roads. Wages fell and prices soared. Poor people suffered the most.

STREET CHILDREN

Over 16 million children now live on the streets of Brazil's largest cities. By day they beg, steal, or earn a little money running errands, sorting through rubbish or washing cars. At night, they sleep rough wherever they can find shelter.

Living on the streets is very dangerous. City businessmen pay 'death squads' of off-duty policemen to 'clean up' the streets by killing robbers and street children. Few of the policemen are ever arrested and punished for their crimes.

▲ Street children in Salvador.

RICH NATION, POOR PEOPLE

During the 1990s, Brazilian governments succeeded in controlling soaring prices. However, there are still 'two Brazils' – one rich, one poor. Most of the country's wealth lies in the hands of just a few people. The poor and the environment suffer. As the map below shows, most farmland is used to grow crops for selling rather than crops for eating.

▼ This map shows the different types of work in Brazil. Most industry is in the south-east.

KEY

- Manufacturing of cars, weapons, machinery and equipment.
- Coffee, sugar cane, rice, soya and oranges farmed and beef cattle reared.
- Plantations of sugar cane, coconuts, bananas and tobacco.
- Plantations of sugar cane and cotton, manioc and tomatoes farmed and cattle reared.
- Cattle ranching and crops grown for selling.
- Cattle ranching and crops grown for eating.
- Pigs and chicken reared, wheat, poatoes, soya, maize and vines farmed.
- Soya, maize, wheat, rice and manioc farmed.
- Small rainforest gardens and farms growing crops for eating.

THE NORTH-EAST: POOREST REGION

NORTH-EAST FACTS

- Covers 20% of Brazil
- 29% of population
- Climate: varied
- Economy: poorest region

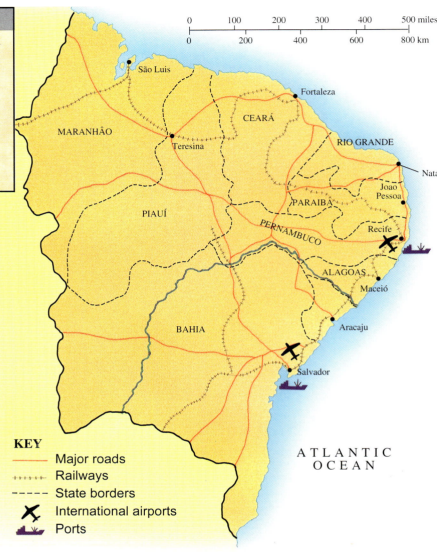

KEY
- Major roads
- Railways
- State borders
- International airports
- Ports

▲ These buildings were built in colonial times.

The north-east was the first part of Brazil to be colonized by Europeans. During early colonial times, sugar cane and other crops made the north-east rich, but later it became poorer. Today it is Brazil's poorest region.

LITTLE INDUSTRY

One of the main reasons the north-east is so poor is that little industry has grown in the region. Most people still live and work in the countryside, working on plantations or on small farms. There are several large cities, but since there is little industry, there are few city jobs.

▲ This woman, from Bahia, is wearing a traditional costume.

AFRICAN TRADITIONS

The north-east has a large black population. Many African traditions, including music and religion, have survived. The region is known as 'the soul of Brazil' because of its colourful culture.

A Candomblé ▶ church parade. The Candomblé religion blends African and Catholic beliefs.

BRAZIL'S SUGAR INDUSTRY

Sugar cane has been an important crop for Brazil since colonial times. The Portuguese established large sugar plantations in the 1500s, and made their fortunes selling processed sugar to Europe.

During the late 1600s, the demand for Brazil's sugar fell because European farmers found out how to produce their own sugar from sugar beet.

In the 1970s, Brazil's sugar made a comeback. Experts found that sugar could be used as a fuel to run motor vehicles. This fuel is called ethanol. Oil had become so expensive, it was cheaper to use ethanol.

Today, all petrol used in cars in Brazil has to contain 20 per cent ethanol. This helps to reduce the amount of oil Brazil must buy in from abroad.

▲The petrol from this pump contains ethanol, or sugar-cane alcohol.

Workers on a ▶
sugar-cane
plantation.

Brazil's sugar is now in demand again, but the lives of workers on the plantations are still very hard. They are very badly paid for long hours of work.

Maria José Trajano da Silva is a sugar-cane worker in the north-east. She works from 5 am until 5 pm, with a two-hour break. She only earns the equivalent of about £1.80 a week.

Women are paid less than men in the plantations. Male workers earn about £2.40 a week for exactly the same work.

It takes a worker about two days to earn enough to buy a kilogram of beans to eat, and three days to buy 2 kilograms of sugar, or a bottle of cooking oil. Maria José Trajano has four children. They don't get enough to eat.

'We are eating only manioc flour. There are no beans to buy now. The hunger is tremendous.' – **Maria José Trajano, sugar-cane worker.**

FARMERS IN THE NORTH-EAST

For most farmers in the north-east, life is a struggle. Plantation owners take the best land near the coast to grow sugar, coffee and tobacco. Sometimes the farmers are violently forced off their land by thugs, hired by rich landowners.

Farmers are pushed on to the hills and plateaus inland, where there is poor soil and it is too dry to grow crops. Some grow beans and cotton, but most graze cattle.

▲ A farmer and his sons at work.

TOURISM AND OIL

In recent years, the growth of tourism and the oil industry have offered new hope to the north-east. Holiday resorts have been built along the coast, where there are thousands of miles of tropical beaches.

Oil was recently discovered offshore in the southern state of Bahia. Oil rigs and refineries have been built, and Bahia now supplies 80 per cent of Brazil's petrol.

These traditional ▶ fishing boats are still used by fishermen in the north-east.

THE SOUTH-EAST: RICHEST REGION

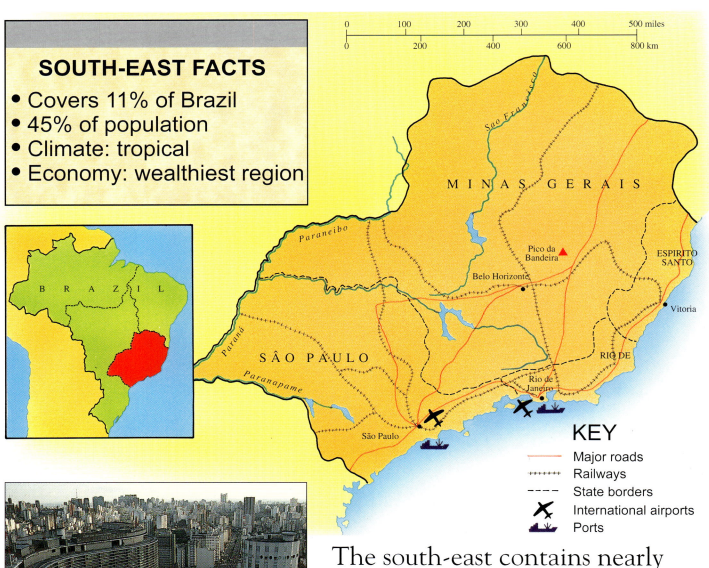

SOUTH-EAST FACTS

- Covers 11% of Brazil
- 45% of population
- Climate: tropical
- Economy: wealthiest region

0   100   200   300   400   500 miles
0   200   400   600   800 km

MINAS GERAIS

B R A Z I L

Paraneibo

Paraná

SÃO PAULO

Paranapame

São Francisco

Pico da Bandeira

Belo Horizonte

ESPIRITO SANTO

Vitoria

RIO DE

Rio de Janeiro

São Paulo

KEY

— Major roads
+++++ Railways
- - - State borders
✕ International airports
⚓ Ports

▲ Skyscrapers tower over the centre of São Paulo.

The south-east contains nearly half of Brazil's population, even though it is only a tenth of the country. Brazil's three largest cities, São Paulo, Rio de Janeiro and Belo Horizonte, all lie here.

A RICH LAND

The south-east is Brazil's wealthiest region. Big plantations, industrial centres and service industries earn a lot of money for the region. Oranges, sugar cane and coffee are major crops. Brazil is the world's leading coffee-producer, and supplies 85 per cent of the world's orange juice.

LAS CLINICAS HOSPITAL

Las Clinicas Hospital in São Paulo is the largest hospital in South America. It spends millions of dollars a month on services and equipment.

In 1993 alone, over 800,000 patients were treated at Las Clinicas. Doctors and scientists from all over the world visit the hospital to do medical research.

A heart ▶ operation at Las Clinicas is checked on high-tech equipment.

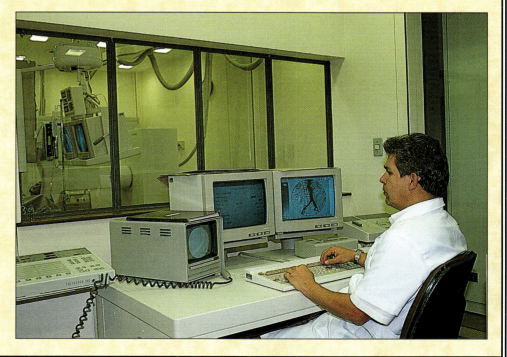

CARNIVAL TIME

Tourism is a major industry in the south-east. One of Brazil's most famous attractions are its carnivals. Carnivals take place all over Brazil in the week before Lent. The most famous is the Rio Carnival, which attracts thousands of tourists.

The Rio Carnival is made up of three parts: street parties, balls and the samba parade. Samba is Brazilian carnival music. During the parade, thousands of musicians and dancers ride through the streets on huge decorated floats. The best display wins a prize.

▼ Around 150 million orange trees grow in the state of São Paulo.

SOCIAL CONDITIONS

Unfortunately, most people in the south-east do not benefit from the region's wealth. Millions of people live in slums, called *favelas*, in the cities. The *favelas* of Rio de Janeiro alone hold over a million people.

The *favela* of Rocinha, in Rio, has at least 60,000 people living in shacks. There is no running water and no sewage system.

THE *FAVELAS*

Despite the wealth of the south-east, the region has thousands of *favelas* or slums. Rio de Janeiro has nearly 500 *favelas*. Over a quarter of the city's population lives there.

Every year, thousands of poor Brazilians leave the countryside to seek work in the cities. The high price of houses means that finding a place to live is very difficult. Most newcomers end up in the slums.

Maria Aparecida de Cavalho lives in a *favela* in São Paulo. She has two children of her own, and has adopted four more because their parents had no money to look after them. She gets some money from a local charity but mainly earns a living by washing clothes.

▲ Maria Aparecida washes clothes in the *favela*.

'There are only two sinks with running water for everyone in the *favela*.' – **Maria Aparecide de Cavalho.**

A few rich people in the south-east enjoy most of the region's wealth. They live in fashionable homes in wealthy suburbs, with ten to fifteen servants and a luxury car.

INDUSTRY AND MINING

The south-east is Brazil's biggest industrial region. The area holds some of the country's richest mines, producing gold, iron ore and other minerals. In the early 1700s, the state of Minas Gerais held the world's richest gold mine.

▲ Brazil's motor industry is one of the world's largest. It produces over a million vehicles each year.

The factories of the south-east produce cars, weapons, electrical equipment, tools and machinery. Hydroelectric plants on the rivers generate power for industry.

Brazil's main industrial region is centred on the city of São Paulo. The motor industry there is the largest in South America, and the ninth-largest in the world. The industry began in the late 1950s. Now international companies such as Volkswagen and Ford have factories there, and the industry employs over 18 per cent of the area's workers.

POLLUTION
The industries of the south-east have their drawbacks. Factories cause serious pollution. The São Paulo district is said to be one of the most polluted places on earth. The pollution affects the health of local children.

▼ The factories around São Paulo create a lot of pollution.

THE NORTH: AMAZON REGION

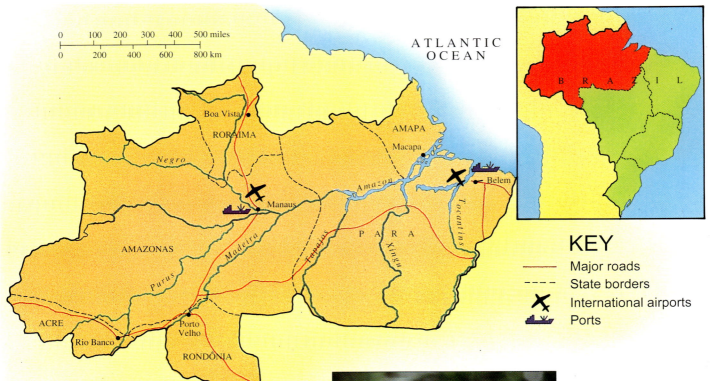

0 100 200 300 400 500 miles
0 200 400 600 800 km

ATLANTIC OCEAN

Boa Vista
RORAIMA
Negro
AMAPA
Macapa
Amazon
Belem
Manaus
Tocantins
AMAZONAS
Madeira
P A R A
Tapajós
Xingu
Purus
ACRE
Porto Velho
Rio Banco
RONDÔNIA

B R A Z I L

KEY
— Major roads
- - - State borders
✕ International airports
🚢 Ports

NORTH FACTS
- Covers 42% of Brazil
- 8% of population
- Climate: humid, with heavy rainfall
- Economy: based on natural resources, including timber, palm fruits, Brazil nuts, iron ore, bauxite, gold and diamonds.

▲ The Amazon rain forest contains an amazing variety of plant and animal species, including monkeys.

The north is Brazil's largest region, but it contains few people. Much of the region is covered by the Amazon rain forest. The Amazon basin is a low-lying area, and large parts of it flood each year.

AMAZON PEOPLES

Most of Brazil's Amerindians live in the Amazon. Once there were millions, but over the centuries, thousands have died of disease or have been killed by settlers moving into the area. Today, there are only a few large groups, or nations.

▲ This waiter works in a hotel in the city of Belem, near the mouth of the Amazon.

Large numbers of *caboclos* also live in the Amazon. These are people of mixed race, who are descended from Amerindians and Europeans. They live a simple life by the rivers, hunting, fishing and gathering fruits.

The largest group in the Amazon are recent settlers from other parts of Brazil. They have moved there in search of a better life.

31

▲ An Amerindian family sifts manioc flour on to a large iron pan to toast it.

ECONOMY

The Amazon holds rich natural resources, including rainforest plants and minerals. It was these resources which first attracted settlers to the region. For generations, Amerindans used and traded forest products.

BRAZIL NUTS

Brazil nuts are the fruit of giant Brazil-nut trees, which grow up to 64 metres high. Mauro Mutran makes his living by selling Brazil nuts abroad. He buys the nuts from Amerindians and *caboclos*, who gather them by hand in the rain forest.

Brazil nuts are popular in Europe. If the price of nuts falls, however, it becomes hard to make a living dealing in the nuts. Mauro Mutran fears the forest will be cut down if the nut market collapses.

MINING AND LOGGING

In 1967, the world's largest deposit of iron ore was discovered in the Carajas mountains in the Amazon. Carajas now lies at the heart of a major mining and farming region.

Copper, gold and cassiterite, the source of tin, are mined there. Factories smelt iron, and there are also large timber plantations.

The developed area is the size of Britain and France put together. All of this huge region was once untouched forest.

▲ Freshly cut logs from a timber plantation in Carajas.

The Amerindians knew how to use the rain forest's resources without harming it. But over the last 300 years, new settlers have done a lot of damage.

Many of the first settlers came to harvest rubber from rubber trees. Cities such as Manaus and Belem became wealthy through rubber. Now large areas of forest have been logged for timber, and huge areas have been cleared for cattle ranches.

FRUITS OF THE FOREST

The Amazon contains over 40,000 different kinds of plants, including thousands of species of trees. The fruits, nuts and berries of the forest provide a source of income for people in the rain forest.

Combu Island lies on the Guama river, a few kilometres from the city of Belem. Orivaldo Quaresma lives on the island. He collects the fruit of the açai palm. He climbs the trees to harvest thousands of purple berries. Then he sells the fruit in markets in Belem.

Orivaldo earns a good living selling açai berries to people who make fruit juice and ice cream. He makes up to £2,000 a year selling açai and cocoa.

Orivaldo's way of life is proof that people can make a living from the rain forest without harming the environment.

'Climbing the açai palm trees isn't easy, but the fruit from a single tree is worth more money than I can earn working for a week in Belem.'
- **Orivaldo Quaresma.**

◀ Orivaldo climbs an açai palm to harvest the berries (shown in detail on the left).

▲ An Amerindian boy waiting to spear a fish. Fish is an important food for people living along the Amazon.

GOLD MINING IN THE AMAZON

In the 1980s, gold was discovered in the Amazon. Thousands of gold-seekers rushed to the region. Today half a million miners work in the area. They disturb the local people and pollute the rivers in their search for gold.

The miners use mercury to separate gold from the mud. Mercury is highly poisonous. Now large amounts of mercury are being poured into the rivers, where it poisons the fish. When the people who live along the rivers eat the fish, they are poisoned too.

CENTRE-WEST: THE WILD WEST

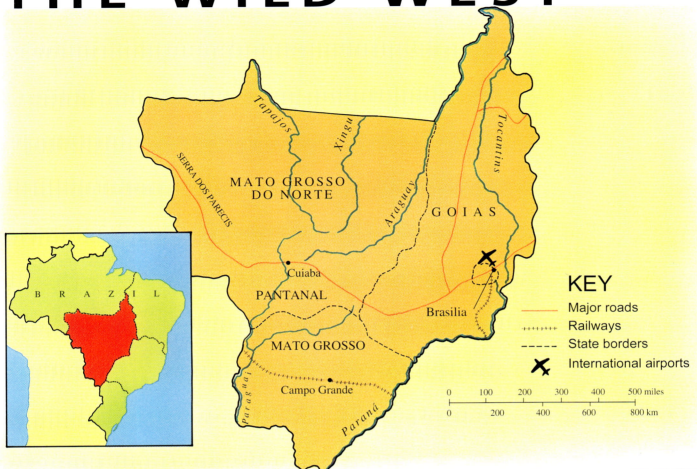

MATO GROSSO DO NORTE

GOIAS

Cuiaba

PANTANAL

Brasilia

MATO GROSSO

Campo Grande

Tapajos

Xingu

Tocantins

Araguay

SERRA DOS PARECIS

Paraguai

Paraná

BRAZIL

KEY
— Major roads
+++++ Railways
- - - State borders
✕ International airports

```
0    100   200   300   400   500 miles
0      200     400     600     800 km
```

CENTRE-WEST FACTS

- Covers 21% of Brazil
- 6% of population
- Climate: tropical, with distinct wet and dry seasons
- Economy: based on farming, ranching, mining and service industries

▲ Many roads in the centre-west are still not paved.

▲ Soya beans are grown and cattle are raised in the Mato Grosso region of western Brazil.

The centre-west is Brazil's second-largest region, yet it holds only a small population. Much of the area is high plateau-land cut by rivers. The region is often called 'the wild west'. Paved roads have only been built there in the last twenty years.

TAMING THE 'WILD WEST'

The centre-west was once home to many Amerindian peoples. Few settlers lived there until the early 1700s, when gold was discovered near Cuiabá. Miners soon flooded in and the population grew quickly. Later settlers were encouraged to move to the west to relieve crowding on the coasts. Nowadays about 10,000 newcomers arrive each year.

THE PANTANAL

The Pantanal is one of the world's great wildernesses. It is a region of swampland the size of France, found on Brazil's western border.

The Pantanal is home to many different animal species. It is one of Brazil's main tourist attractions. Visitors come to see alligators, jaguars, deer, monkeys and capybaras. Over 600 species of birds also live there, and over 350 different fish, including flesh-eating piranhas, swim in its rivers.

▲ During the rainy season, much of the Pantanal is flooded. Many waterbirds live there.

MINERS AND COWBOYS

Settlers first moved to the centre-west in search of gold and also Amerindian slaves. There is still mining, but most of the region's money is now made through farming and cattle ranching. The main crops grown are maize, rice and soya beans. The centre-west is home to the world's largest soya-bean farm.

Large herds of beef cattle graze the centre-west's rolling grasslands. They are rounded up by cowboys known as gauchos. Valuable hardwood trees also grow in the region and are logged for timber.

BRASILIA

The city of Brasilia, in the centre-west, is Brazil's capital. Yet it has only existed since 1960.

Brasilia was built in 1960, because Brazilians wanted their capital to be in the centre of their country.

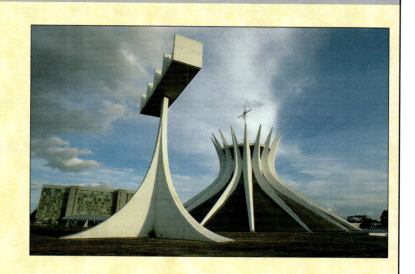

The city was built in less than four years. This was an amazing achievement since there were no road or railways nearby. All the workers and supplies had to be flown in by plane.

Brasilia contains many beautiful modern buildings, but the designers did not allow space for the city to grow. Temporary houses on the outskirts, which were built for builders, are now home to the city's poor. The centre of Brasilia has plenty of space, but it has been designed for cars rather than people on foot.

▲ This is Brasilia's modern cathedral.

▼ Poor workers live in *favelas* on the city outskirts.

THE SOUTH: SMALLEST REGION

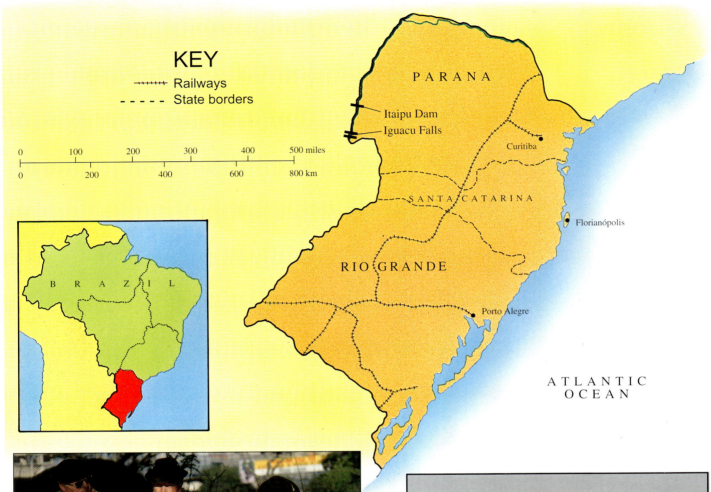

KEY

+++++++ Railways

- - - - - State borders

0   100   200   300   400   500 miles

0   200   400   600   800 km

BRAZIL

PARANA

Itaipu Dam
Iguacu Falls

Curitiba

SANTA CATARINA

Florianópolis

RIO GRANDE

Porto Alegre

ATLANTIC OCEAN

▲ People wear warm clothes on a frosty morning in the south.

SOUTH FACTS

- Covers 7% of Brazil

- 16% of population

- Climate: humid and subtropical, with four seasons

- Economy: wealthy, based on farming.

▲ The Iguaçu Falls are one of the world's largest and most beautiful waterfalls.

The south is Brazil's smallest region, but it has a large population. The climate there is cooler than the rest of Brazil, with four seasons, like Britain.

PEOPLE OF THE SOUTH

The south once held many Amerindian peoples. Thousands were kidnapped by slave traders. Others were taken by missionaries, trying to convert them to Christianity.

Since colonial times, the fertile lands of the south have attracted large numbers of settlers from European and Middle Eastern countries, including Germany, Italy, Poland, Russia and Syria.

LIVING CONDITIONS

The south is a wealthy area. People there generally have better living standards than elsewhere in Brazil. However, because of problems in other regions, large numbers of poor people are now heading south.

ECONOMY

The economy of the south is based on farming and cattle ranching. Chickens and pigs are also reared. The main crops grown are wheat, coffee, grapes, soya beans, potatoes and a herbal tea called *maté*. There are also large plantations of pine trees, and coal mining is an important industry.

BRAZILIAN WINE

The southern state of Rio Grande do Sul is famous for its vineyards. The region produces 90 per cent of Brazil's wine.

The main wine-makers are the descendants of Italian settlers. The climate and the landscape of the region are similar to southern Italy.

Today the area has a distinctly Italian feel. Traditional Italian cheeses and sausages hang from the ceilings of wine cellars.

Once, Brazilian wines were produced only for Brazilians to drink. Now Brazil sells almost as much fine wine as its neighbours, Chile and Argentina.

▲ A wine cellar in Rio Grande do Sul.

▲ Itaipu Dam is the site of the world's largest hydroelectric power plant. The project flooded a huge area of land above the dam.

THE PARANÁ RIVER

The mighty Paraná river runs along the border with Paraguay and Argentina. At Iguaçu Falls, the river drops 72 metres in a series of spectacular waterfalls. The site is a major tourist attraction.

Only 10 miles from Iguaçu, a giant dam has been built to generate electricity from the fast-flowing river. Itaipu Dam was built between 1975 and 1991, at the cost of £15 billion. Supporters of the project say the electricity was needed for region's industries. But many people say it has caused great damage to the environment.

BRAZIL'S FUTURE

Brazil is lucky to have rich natural resources and great mineral wealth. Over the last 40 years, the country has industrialized quickly. Now it has many manufactured goods to sell abroad, as well as minerals and farm products.

DEBT AND SOCIAL CONDITIONS

Brazil developed its industries using money borrowed from abroad. Now it has the biggest debt of any developing country. Recent governments have begun to pay the money back. But they have had to spend less on public services to do so.

▼ Large families are common in Brazil. Nearly half the population is under 20 years old.

The result is that living conditions for many Brazilians have got worse. For example, schools are badly funded, with not enough teachers or classrooms.

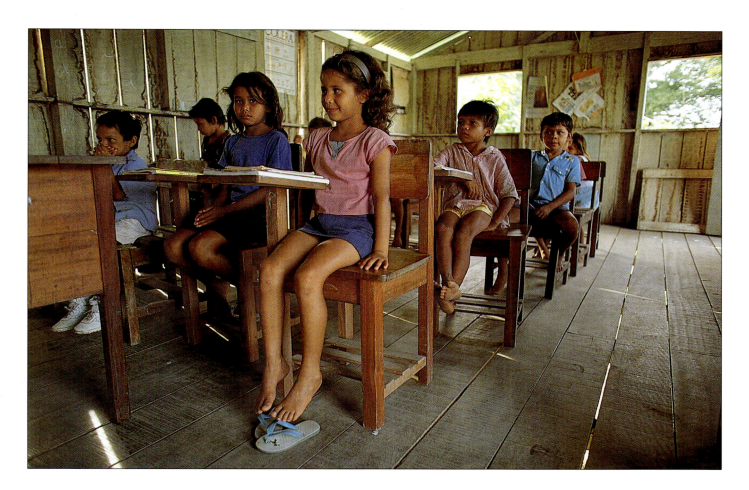

▲ The goverment needs to spend more money on schools in the future.

Most Brazilians get poor medical care. Many people die of infectious diseases or from drinking dirty water. Others starve to death. Many babies die at birth.

Brazil has many thriving industries. But only a small fraction of the population enjoys the profits. Most people live in poverty, in crowded *favelas* or poor country areas. In future, Brazil must work towards a fairer society, in which the environment is respected, and the country's land and wealth are shared out more equally.

GLOSSARY

Amerindian The first people known to have lived in South America. They have lived on the continent for thousands of years.

Colony A country that is controlled by another country, which is usually more rich and powerful.

Crops Plants such as wheat or cotton that have been specially grown to be harvested.

Debts Sums of money owed to another person or country.

Discriminate To treat someone unfairly because of their race, colour, religion or sex.

Economy The wealth of a country.

Favela A slum in Brazil.

Gaucho Cowboy from South America.

Gross Domestic Product The size of a country's economy. It is based on the total value of goods a country produces for sale within its own borders.

Hydroelectricity Electricity generated by harnessing the power of fast-flowing water.

Immigrants People who arrive from a foreign country to settle.

Independence When a country becomes free from foreign rule.

Industrialize Increase the number of industries.

Loans Sums of money that have been borrowed.

Manioc A root vegetable that can be ground up and made into flour to bake bread.

Manufacturing Making goods.

Natural resources Plants that can be harvested to make money for people, such as timber, minerals and food crops.

Plantations Large farms which produce a single crop such as sugar cane, coffee or bananas.

Plateau An area of raised land.

Slums Poor, overcrowded housing.

Tropical Belonging to the Tropics, the zone on either side of the Equator, between the Tropics of Cancer and Capricorn.

Tropical climate A climate with high temperatures and abundant rainfall, found in the Tropics.

TOPIC WEB

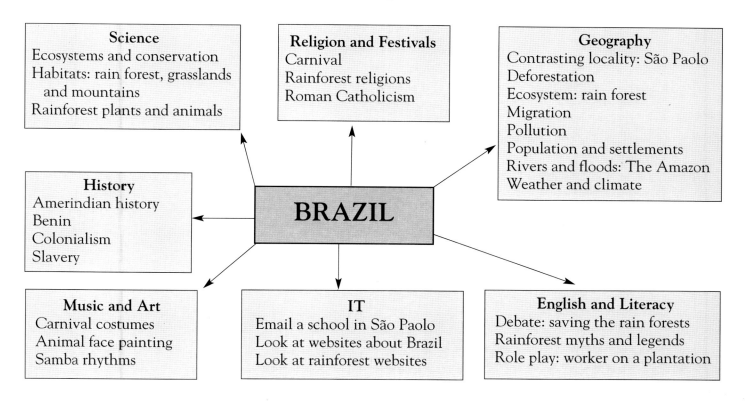

Science
Ecosystems and conservation
Habitats: rain forest, grasslands
  and mountains
Rainforest plants and animals

Religion and Festivals
Carnival
Rainforest religions
Roman Catholicism

Geography
Contrasting locality: São Paolo
Deforestation
Ecosystem: rain forest
Migration
Pollution
Population and settlements
Rivers and floods: The Amazon
Weather and climate

History
Amerindian history
Benin
Colonialism
Slavery

BRAZIL

Music and Art
Carnival costumes
Animal face painting
Samba rhythms

IT
Email a school in São Paolo
Look at websites about Brazil
Look at rainforest websites

English and Literacy
Debate: saving the rain forests
Rainforest myths and legends
Role play: worker on a plantation

FINDING OUT MORE

BOOKS AND PHOTOPACKS

Antonio's Rain Forest by Anna Lewington
(Wayland, 1995)

Brazil (*Country Insights* series) by Eddie
Parker (Wayland, 1997)

Carnival (*Festivals* series) by Clare Chandler
(Wayland, 1996)

A Flavour of Brazil by Mariana Serra
(Wayland, 1999)

People of the Rain Forest by Eddie Parker
(Wayland, 1998)

South America (*Continents* series) (Wayland,
1997)

Stories from the Amazon by Saviour Pirotta
(Wayland, 1999)

Worldfocus: Brazil by David Marshall
(Heinemann, 1997)

ADDRESSES AND WEBSITES

ActionAid, Hamlyn House, Archway,
London N19 5PG. Tel 0207 282 4101
Website: www.actionaid.org

Brazilian Embassy, 32 Green Street, London
W1Y 4AT.

Brazil Network, PO Box 1325, London SW9
6BG.

Living Earth Foundation, Warwick House,
106 Harrow Road, London W2 1XD.

Oxfam: 274 Banbury Road, Oxford OX2
7DZ. Tel: 01865 56777
Website: www.oxfam.org.uk

Development Education Association, 3rd
Floor, Cowper Street, London EC2A 4AP

Unicef: 55-6 Lincoln's Inn Fields, London
WC2A 3NB. Tel: 0207 405 5592
Email: info@unicef.org.uk

INDEX

Page numbers in **bold** show pictures as well as text.